I0190595

Season Of Joy

Dramas For Advent — Christmas — Epiphany

C.S.S. Publishing Company, Inc.
Lima, Ohio

SEASON OF JOY

Copyright © 1991 by
The C.S.S. Publishing Company, Inc.
Lima, Ohio

You may copy the material in this publication if you are the original purchaser, for use as it was intended (worship material for worship use; educational material for classroom use; dramatic material for staging and production). No additional permission is required from the publisher for such copying by the original purchaser only. Inquiries should be addressed to: The C.S.S. Publishing Company, Inc., 628 South Main Street, Lima, Ohio 45804.

9152 / ISBN 1-55673-353-4   PRINTED IN U.S.A.

TABLE OF CONTENTS

These Things Belong To Christmas
(For Advent Or Christmas)

Production Notes   7

Order Of Service   8

Scene 1   10
    The Prophet, Isaiah's Monologue

Scene 2   12
    Children Reach Out

Scene 3   15
    Lonely? Not Really

Scene 4   17
    Gifts

Scene 5   19
    Trimming The Tree

Scene 6   21
    Christmas Is Worship

Three Gifts of Love
(For Christmas Or Epiphany)

Production Notes   27

Act I — Scene 1   29

Scene 2   31

Scene 3   33

Act II — Scene 1   34

Scene 2   38

These Things Belong To Christmas

A play for Advent or Christmas

By Emmeline S. Miller
and Char Schultz

PRODUCTION NOTES

This program was planned so that part or all of it could be used for an evening service during Advent or for Christmas. It requires few properties: a couch or davenport, card table, several chairs, Palestinian costume, and Bible, paper and pen.

Scenes 1 and 2 can be played on the front of the stage. For scenes 3, 4, 5, 6, the living room furniture should be moved forward.

Performance time: (not counting singing of hymns) 20-25 minutes.

THESE THINGS
BELONG TO CHRISTMAS

Suggested Order Of Service

Prelude:

Christmas carol medley

Hymn: "O Come, O Come, Emmanuel"

Leader: Celebrate Christmas with us as we hear from the prophet, Isaiah. He foretold the coming of Christ many years before Christ was born.

Scene 1: Isaiah's Monologue — The Prophet

Leader: We are told to receive the gift of salvation as little children. Let's watch now as the children plan to give the gift of love to an old friend. They are walking home from school as we look at this scene.

Scene 2: Children Reach Out

Leader: There's one gift that keeps on giving — it's the love of Christ as he lives in each of us. Listen to this message as it is sung by the children.

Hymn: "Away In a Manger" — Children's choir

Leader: Those who are alone and away from family and friends need to feel the love and presence of Christ. But can that be sent by mail? Let's see;

Scene 3: Lonely? Not Really

Hymn:	"We Three Kings"
Leader:	Giving something special to those we love is a part of Christmas that touches all of us. Sometimes we lose our perspective as you will see in this next scene.
Scene 4:	Gifts
Hymn:	"O Christmas Tree"
Leader:	On a lighter note decorating the tree is a highlight for children and adults. Let's watch and enjoy as one of our church families shows us how to trim the tree properly.
Scene 5:	Trimming The Tree
Leader:	During this holy season we realize that we are worshiping a special king who lives and reigns in our hearts today. Two families will now join to celebrate Christmas in a unique and wonderful way. They hope the audience will join in singing the hymns.
Scene 6:	Christmas Is Worship
Benediction:	Pastor

ISAIAH'S MONOLOGUE
– THE PROPHET

Scene 1

I am Isaiah, a priest and prophet of Israel.
I was born in the year 760 B.C. in the beautiful city of Jerusalem. That was 2,700 years ago.
My uncle, Uzziah was king at that time. I was proud of him for he was a good king who ruled for almost 20 years. Israel prospered under him and the land was rich and the food was plentiful.
When I was in my late teens Uncle Uzziah died. There was sadness and confusion in Jerusalem and the gates of the temple built by Solomon were left unguarded. Seeking some spiritual strength I quietly crept into the temple.
The beauty of the temple so overwhelmed me my eyes were filled with tears. Suddenly through my tears I saw the Lord sitting upon his throne with his beautiful garment filling the temple. Then it seemed that the whole room was filled with smoke and the pillars seemed to shake. Perhaps it was I shaking, rather than the pillars.
I felt so unworthy to be in such a beautiful place, I cried out, "O Lord, I have unclean lips and am unworthy to be in your house." But then it seemed that an angel appeared and took a coal of fire from the altar and touched my lips and whispered, "Your sins are forgiven."
Suddenly I heard a voice echoing through the halls, asking, "Who will go for me and do my work?" I immediately answered, "Here am I; send me." I left that room determined to give my life to the priesthood.
I was accepted as a priest. For 40 years I served in Jerusalem both as a priest and as a prophet. One of the dreams I received from the Lord was: "And the government shall be upon his shoulders and his name shall be called wonderful Counselor, mighty God, everlasting Father, Prince of Peace."

I did not know who this would be, but the Lord went on to say: "The wolf shall dwell with the lamb and the leopard shall lie down with the kid and the calf and the lion shall eat together, and a little child shall lead them. . . . And they shall beat their swords into plowshares and their spears into pruning hooks. Nations shall not learn war anymore."

This beautiful dream of a warless world never came true in my lifetime. Perhaps some day it will be fulfilled. For the Lord has promised it.

(Isaiah should be dressed in Palestinian costume.)

CHILDREN REACH OUT

Scene 2

(This skit used four children, ages 11, 12, or 13. Two are walking home from school with books in hand. They are joined by the other two who run to catch up with them.)

First child: Only 23 more days until Christmas — I can't wait.

Second child: Only 15 more days until vacation. Homework! Homework!

First child: What do you do on Christmas, stay home or visit relatives?

Second child: We stay home. I love playing with all my presents. I want a computer with software, a track certified dirt bike and an official soccer ball — orange and black.

First Child: Your list is long. I like both money and presents, then I can buy what I want after Christmas.

Second child: Well, you can't play with money on Christmas day. I mean Christmas is presents, isn't it?

(Children three and four join the other two)

Third child: Oh, hi, everyone! What are you talking about?

First child: Christmas, of course.

Second child: What do you want?

Third child: Well, I want clothes, books, and a few toys.

Second child: Toys are okay, but books and clothes?

Fourth child: I have an idea I want to talk to you about. Do you remember Mrs. Smith, the old lady who lives on Main Street, who was always working in her yard when we walked by on our way to school this fall?

All: Yes.

First child: She had the most beautiful flowers and always had a smile and a cheerful "Hello" when we walked by her yard.

Second child: Where is she? I haven't seen her lately?

Fourth child: My mom told me that she is at the nursing home. She fell and broke her hip. The worst part is she's all alone. Her husband died last year and she never had any children.

First child: I guess we were like her grandchildren. Remember the day we went up on her porch for cookies and milk after school?

Second child: Yeah, I always thought old ladies hated children until I met her.

Fourth child: In Sunday school we were talking about the real meaning of Christmas — giving, not getting. I was thinking about all the smiles and happiness she has given us.

All: Yeah.

First child: Can kids our age visit at the nursing home?

Second child: A friend of mine has.

First child: Let's go visit Mrs. Smith some afternoon after our vacation starts.

Third child: We could bake cookies to take to her. My mom lets me mess up the kitchen all the time.

First child: I have a small artificial Christmas tree we could take and decorate there.

Second child: Let's each make a special ornament to decorate as well as several balls from our own tree.

First child: We could sing carols for her also.

Fourth child: Great! All I wanted was for us to visit Mrs. Smith, but with all your suggestions this is going to be the neatest thing we have ever done. It will be a Christmas we will never forget.

(Children exit, laughing)

LONELY? NOT REALLY

Scene 3

(Nurse enters pushing an elderly lady in a wheelchair)

Nurse: I'm new here, what is your name?

Patient: My name is Mary — Mary Dolittle — I tell folks who come to visit me, because that suits me — you know Dolittle? Names are no longer important to me. There was a time — but you didn't come here to hear my life story. You're too busy for that. Did you bring me something?

Nurse: Your mail. There seems to be a lot of Christmas cards for you, you must have many friends. *(Hands cards to Mary)*

Patient: Let's see if I can guess who sent them. *(Picks up one and looks at envelope)* It's postmarked New York and the return address says Thomas Brown. *(Opens envelope)* He was that red-haired freckle-faced boy whom I taught in seventh grade, I believe. Never could keep him quiet. *(reads)* "I'm performing in a play on Broadway and I wanted you to know your insistence on pronunciation and good English have helped me to get this far in my chosen field. Thank you and have a Merry Christmas." Well, now, who would have thought he would become a successful actor. How good of him to remember me at Christmas.

(Picks up another card) Florida? Jennifer Jones? *(Opens it)* I can't remember — *(Reads card aloud)* "I doubt if you remember me but I used to live down the street from you. One year when my mother was ill you baked us cookies for Christmas. I just learned that you were in a nursing

15

home and since I can't visit you I'm sending this card for old times' sake. Have a blessed Christmas, 'Neighbor.' "

Now I remember her and her family — but that was 30 years ago. She never forgot!

(Looks at another) This one didn't come very far, just from Grove City — oh, it's from my old friend, Merle. We used to travel to meetings together with our husbands. What happy times we had! Wonder what she will say — *(Opens and reads).* "Shut your eyes and travel with me to the top of the St. Louis arch. Remember we stood in line for one hour and then you got claustrophobia and wanted to rush back down after we got up there. What fun we had! My old broken down body wouldn't let me visit you but I can visit in spirit. Merry Christmas — love you!"

(Chuckles) Good old Merle!

(Picks up another) Here's one from Dayton, Ohio. *(Opens and reads)* Our son and daughter will be with us this Christmas so we will not be able to visit you. Be assured you will be remembered as we gather around the table. Your gracious hospitality and friendship during the years they were in college in your town added so much to their lives as well as to ours. Our thoughts and prayers will include you.

(Sits quietly and looks at rest of the greetings) Goodness — it will take all day to read all of these; each one brings back a different chapter in my life. It was a full life and now, now I can sit back and reap the harvest in thought. Lonely? Not really, I'm never alone. God is good.

(Falls asleep. Letters drop to floor.)

Nurse: *(Enters, picks up cards)* Bless her — she's fallen asleep. From the smile on her face her cards must have cheered her. *(Tiptoes out)*

GIFTS

Scene 4

Mom: *(Enters loaded with packages from an evening's shopping)* Are the children asleep?

Dad: *(Reading the paper, stretched out on the davenport)* Yes, they've been sleeping for about a half hour.

Mom: Let's see, I got your sister finished and my dad and your mother. I have no idea what to buy for my mother. She always says get me some perfume and a nice card. Just once I'd like to surprise her but she has everything she needs and wants. I still haven't started to shop for the kids — one minute it's the Ewok village and the next it's a Knight Rider car. Last week it was the Lego castle. It's no use buying ahead because right up to Christmas Eve they are changing their minds. What can I buy for your dad?

Dad: What did you say, dear? *(Continues to read the paper)*

Mom: I said, What can I buy for your dad?

Dad: Whatever you decide is fine.

Mom: *(Sarcastically)* Whatever you decide is fine. You pull this trick on me each year. I'm the one stuck with all the shopping, all the cleaning, all the cooking, and all the decorating. What do you do — read the paper!

Dad: *(finally sits up and lays down the paper)* You're a much better shopper than I am. You know I hate to shop. If I do it I'm going to buy the first thing that catches my fancy just to get it over with. I'll just try to pay the bills.

17

By the way what did you pay for all this with — the North Dakota Master Card, the Huntington Master Card or the Columbus Visa?

Mom: What am I supposed to do — they have to have presents — it's Christmas.

Dad: Well, do we have to buy for your great aunt this year? She never likes what we choose.

Mom: It seems to be a vicious cycle. We buy things people don't want or need and they do the same for us. It goes on year after year. The time that we are supposed to be celebrating we're worried about what to buy and how to pay the bills. Our focus is all wrong! How can we change it? *(Turns to audience)* Can you tell us how?

TRIMMING THE TREE

Scene 5

(The scene opens with mom moving the furniture, trying to decide where to place the tree.)

Dad: *(Enters)* Can you believe that we spent three hours looking for the perfect tree? Don't you think that driving to five Christmas tree lots and two tree farms to cut your own tree is a little ridiculous?

Mom: Well, the tree is important and with all the company we have I want it to look nice.

Dad: It should. When I was a boy a tree this size was $3 and we paid $25 for this one. Times have surely changed.

Mom: *(Shakes her head)* Are you ready to bring it in? I've cleared a spot for it.

Dad: Yes, I just finished putting it on the stand.

Mom: I thought so — you have a bunch of needles in your hair. (Brushes them off) Now when you carry it in try not to crash into the door as you do every year. By the time you get it inside, it's lost a third of its needles.

Dad: Okay! Okay! *(Dad exits — returns with the tree)* Now, where have the children gone? When we bought the tree they were so excited about the prospect of trimming it.

Mom: I'll call them — *(She calls them by name, they run into the room, screaming "Hooray," jumping up and down, quite excited.*

(After all have entered they start decorating the tree from a box filled with ornaments which have been placed on the table. Mom tries to tell them to space the ornaments so that all the tree will be covered. Then after all the ornaments have been used, mom demonstrates to the children how to hang the icicles properly. Dad leaves the room, saying he has to get water for the tree stand. Just then, the phone rings and mom goes to answer it. After both have left the room the children begin to throw the icicles, laughing and giggling at their efforts. By the time mom returns they are finished. Mom looks suspiciously at the tree but says nothing. The children look relieved.)

Smallest child: Look at my side of the tree, Mom. *(He shows her; the ornaments are in one closely knit bunch)*

Mom: Don't you want to spread them out a little?

Boy: No, I like them this way.

Mom: Well, it's time for all of you to get your baths and go to bed. Daddy will take you upstairs. Do I get kisses and hugs? *(The children respond, then exit as Mom says, "See you in the morning.")*
(After the children are gone mom shakes her head as she looks at the tree and then carefully rearranges it to suit herself.)

(This skit was written for a family with five children. The trimming of the tree was unrehearsed.)

20

CHRISTMAS IS WORSHIP

Scene 6

(Elaine is walking across the stage, books on her arm, going home from school. Amy and Michael enter, hurry to overtake her.)

Michael: Elaine, wait.

Elaine: *(Turns, sees them, stops)* Hi, Michael, Amy, what's cooking?

Amy: We have an idea. I guess you know your mother and dad invited our family to come to your house Christmas night. How about you and Michael and I planning a worship service for our two families?

Elaine: That would be fun. When can we do it? That afternoon? Could you two come over early, after you are tired playing with your new games?

Michael: Sure we can, can't we Amy? *(Amy nods)*

Elaine: Okay. Be there by 4 p.m. Think of some good ideas. *(All exit)*

New Scene

(Elaine is seated by a card table, leafing through the Bible. There is pen and paper on the table. There are two other chairs at the table. There is a knock at the door, she goes and admits Amy and Michael. The three seat themselves around the table.)

Elaine: Have you been thinking about what we should do?

Amy: Yes, my dad will read the Scripture. Which one shall we use?

Michael: I want to hear the one about the angels. Where do you find it?

Elaine: Here's a Bible — I think it is in Luke. *(Looks)* Yes, here it is, Luke 2:1-20. Write that down, Amy. *(Amy writes)*

Amy: Can't your mother play the piano for us to sing carols?

Elaine: Sure, I'll ask her but I know she will.

Amy: Why don't you sing a solo, Elaine?

Elaine: Okay. If you will read a poem. Here, I found a short one in a book at school. *(Hands her a copy of the poem)*

Michael: May I be the usher? We could make programs to give to everyone.

Amy: That's a good idea. Now, let's see that just leaves my mom and your dad, Elaine.

Elaine: Who will give the sermon?

Michael: Aw! We don't want a sermon. How about a story?

Elaine: All right. Let's ask your mom to read a story, she knows lots of good ones, and my dad can give the Christmas prayer.
(Looks over program Amy has been writing) There, I think everyone has something to do.

Michael: Can't we have an offering?

Elaine: Why not? We could give it to CROP.

Amy: That's neat. This is going to be the best Christmas ever!
Now we just have to make copies of the program for
everyone.
(They all nod and exit laughing)

New Scene

*(Both families enter, seat themselves as Michael hands out
the program. Elaine presides and announces the various parts
of the program which was planned by the children. The audience joins them in singing the hymns.)*

Christmas Is

Christmas is a lighted tree,
A candle and a star.
Christmas is a stable where
The waiting shepherds are.

Christmas is a carol sung
In frosty winter air.
An angel's wings, a manger bed,
And God's love cradled there.
                              Soule

(Poem to be used in service)

Three Gifts Of Love

A play in two acts for Christmas or Epiphany

by Linda Aranda

PRODUCTION NOTES

Cast: Narrator *(can be omitted)*
Servant
Two Guards
Melchior
Balthazar
Herod's Advisor
Kaspar
King Herod
Chief Priest
Chief Guard
Mary

CHARACTERS: two female, nine male

PLAYING TIME: 25 minutes

COSTUMES: Biblical robes and head pieces. Herod wears royal robe of purple or gold and a crown. Magi wear simple robes and head pieces, beards, sandals or bare feet. In Act II, they need more elaborate robes, but not as "royal" as Herod. Guards wear helmets, breast plates and carry spears.

PROPERTIES: Dish or pitcher for servant, three camel's heads (cardboard) above screen on right, traveling papers with gold seal, couch for Herod, throne or elevated chair, three cushions, lighted star, food on tray, three containers for gold, frankincense, myrrh, cradle, doll.

SETTING: Divide stage into inside and outside separated by columns. Act I, Scenes 1 and 3: Courtyard — plants surround small pond in center (wading pool). Scene 2: couch in center of room, gold wall hangings. Act II, Scene I: throne replaces couch. Scene 2: screens form outline of small house, open in front. Cradle in center front.

LIGHTING: Darken portion of stage not being used OR leave lights as is and spotlight part of stage in use.

SOUNDS: Horses trotting — Act II, Scene 1 and 2.

ACT I

Scene 1

Setting: Outside King Herod's Palace in West Jerusalem.

Narrator: Three dusty, foot-sore travelers near the entrance of Herod's palace. An exhausting journey has left their faces haggard and scorched by the desert sun. Each man is leading a camel laden with only the barest of necessities. Advancing into the courtyard, the men stare hungrily at the scene before them. No, it is not the splendor of Herod's palace that has caught their eye, but the small pond surrounded by lush grass and flowers. One of the three men is drawn to the pond. Stiffly he bends to play with the water, letting its coolness trickle through his fingers.

Servant: *(Hurrying across the courtyard, he stops. Eyeing their dirty, unkempt clothing, he shouts.)* What business do you people have in Herod's court? How did you get in here? Where are the guards? Guards! Guards!
(Two large, burly palace guards come running into the courtyard. They are dressed in helmets and breast plates and carry large spears.)

Servant: Where have you two been? Seize these men! Herod will have your heads!
(The guards grab the two men still standing.)

Melchior: *(Forcing himself upright, away from the water.)* We have come to worship the newly-born King of the Jews.

Servant: *(Puzzled)* Who's that? There's no baby here.

Balthazar: We would like an audience with Herod.

29

Servant: Wait here. I'll get Herod's advisor. *(He leaves.)*

Narrator: Moments later another man enters the courtyard. He seems taken aback by the scene before him. He fakes friendliness.

Advisor: What can I do for you people?

Kaspar: *(Speaks strongly with authority)* We wish an audience with King Herod. We have come to worship the newborn King of the Jews.

Advisor: *(Not quite concealing his amazement)* I see. Do you have traveling papers?

Narrator: The advisor studies the documents for some time before he is convinced of their authenticity. He looks up smiling.

Advisor: Welcome to King Herod's court. Come inside for food, drink and rest. You have journeyed far?

Balthazar: Yes, many months. *(He sighs with weariness.)*

ACT I

Scene 2

Setting: Inside Herod's personal chambers.

Advisor: Sire, three strange men have come to your court asking for the newly-born King of the Jews.

Herod: *(Surprised)* Newly-born what? *(He laughs.)*

Advisor: *(Hurrying on)* Their travel papers are in order and the royal seal is affixed.

Herod: Where are these men, now?

Advisor: I left orders for the servants to care for them. They have come a long way.

Herod: Good. We need time to investigate their presence here. Get the Chief Priest quickly.

(Some time later the Chief Priest enters.)

Chief Priest: How may I serve you, King Herod? *(He bows.)*

Herod: Three strangers have come to the court looking for the newly-born King of the Jews. What do you know of this?

Chief Priest: *(Speaking slowly and carefully)* The ancient prophets tell of such a child to be born in Bethlehem who will be King of the Jews.

Herod: What do you mean King? *(He insists.)* I am the king, here!

Chief Priest: That you are, sire. I am only repeating the words of Jeremiah of our people.

Herod: Yes, yes. *(He dismisses the priest with a wave of his hand.) (To the advisor standing hearby)* Get me the captain of the guard, at once.

Advisor: Yes, sire. *(He rushes out.)*

Narrator: Herod is puzzled and afraid. Like many unpopular kings, he fears assassination and intends to stay in power for many years.

(The Chief Guard enters, bows and kneels.)

Herod: *(Impatiently)* Choose some of your best men. Go into the streets. Find out what the people are talking about. Send others to the surrounding country side. I must know what is on the people's minds!

Chief Guard: *(He rises.)* Yes, sire.

Herod: Use bribery or force if you have to! *(Guard exits.) (Muttering to himself)* How can this be happening and I, the king, not know about it? Someone will pay!

ACT I

Scene 3

Setting: Early evening just as the stars begin to appear in the sky. The three men are walking in the palace courtyard.

Balthazar: Why is Herod making us wait so long? We've been here four days now.

Melchior: The rest has been most welcome. I couldn't have traveled much farther. *(All nod in agreement.)*

Kaspar: But we need to get on about our business.

Balthazar: Surely the king would be happy to share the birth of a new son.

Kaspar: The servants say Herod has children, but there is no baby in the household.

Balthazar: Herod has certainly kept us isolated. We have seen no one but his advisor and a few servants.

Melchior: But Herod has been most generous in providing our needs. I've enjoyed the time here.

Kaspar: Let's not be lulled into inactivity by our pleasant surroundings. Remember our gifts.

Balthazar: *(Pointing)* Look, the stars are in readiness, Jupiter and Saturn are nearing. We must watch for the reappearance of the King's star.

Servant: *(Entering the courtyard behind the three stargazers.)* Excuse me, sirs. King Herod sends word that he will speak with you tomorrow.

Kaspar: At last! We can continue our mission.

ACT II

Scene 1

Narrator: The magi are summoned the next day to Herod's chambers. Herod eyes the three figures closely as they enter. Wearing robes supplied by the servants, they bear little resemblance to the worn travelers of four days before. They are ushered onto several large, brightly-colored cushions, arranged in a semi-circle before Herod's chair.

Herod: I hope you have fared well in my household.

Melchior: Yes, sire. You have made us most welcome. We were exhausted from our journey. As you can see by our gray beards, we are not young men.

Herod: *(In a voice filled with curiosity)* Who are you? What do you seek?

Balthazar: We are the magi, your excellence, astrologers and healers.

Kaspar: Surely you are aware of the significance of the stars.

Herod: Yes, yes. Go on.

Balthazar: A new star appeared in the section of the sky governed by the sign of the fish — the house of the Hebrews.

Melchior: This can only mean that what the ancient tablets foretold is coming true.

Kaspar: You see, whenever two great planets such as Jupiter and Saturn merge, a great event will occur.

(Silence prevails for a few moments before Herod shakes off his thoughts.)

Herod: A new star you say . . . One that never existed before?

Melchior: Yes, sire. And such a star! It blazed up suddenly with a flaming tail!

Kaspar: *(In a hushed tone)* First, a steel-blue spark. Then a crimson sphere intensified to a white radiant star.

(All of the magi gaze silently upward, even in Herod's palace, reliving the wondrous event.)

Balthazar: *(After a few moments, he speaks.)* We followed the star here — over many treacherous miles.

Melchior: Down steep mountain sides, across the shifting sands — we pushed on.

Kaspar: The burning sun scorched us by day and the desert nights chilled our bones.

Melchior: Yet the star pulsated overhead, urging us on.

Kaspar: Barking jackals disturbed our sleep.

Balthazar: Every ravine echoed with the lion's roar.

Melchior: Each night we eagerly awaited the star's rising for courage.

Herod: *(With a hint of sarcasm)* Why, sirs have you come to my court? I am the only king here. Your eyes, however dimmed by age, can see that I am not a babe. Yet, I am the King of the Jews!

(The three exchange silent glances uncertain how to continue after Herod's remark.)

Melchior: We have come to ask your help. Your soldiers patrol the countryside.

Balthazar: Surely nothing happens that the great King Herod is not made aware of.

Herod: What would you do once the king is found? What is your purpose?

Kaspar: *(Slightly amazed at Herod's ignorance)* Why sire, to worship him. To show our adoration by bringing gifts suitable only for a king.

Herod: Gifts — you say?

Melchior: Yes, gold — the symbol of earthly power and might.

Kaspar: I bring frankincense — the purest of all resins — symbolic of holiness and the deity.

Balthazar: Lastly, I bring myrrh — the aromatic salve and bitter spice meaning mortality and death.

Narrator: As the afternoon wears on, the magi become most impatient with Herod's questioning. Their question: if the King is not here, then where . . . occupies their thoughts. They press Herod for information.

Kaspar: *(Leaning toward Herod)* Can you help us, sire?

Melchior: Do your soldiers tell you of such a king?

Herod: *(Leaning back in his chair, pleased with having the upper hand in the situation)* Not my soldiers, but the Jewish high priests. They say the prophets foretold of such a one as you speak of in a small hamlet, five miles hence, Bethlehem.

Narrator: The magi spring to their feet, electrified by the words from Herod's lips. The men prepare to leave even before Herod has dismissed them.

Herod: *(Raising his hands to delay their departure)* Gentlemen, gentlemen, my stables are at your disposal. Choose horses for your use. But you must make a promise to me. When you have found this new king, you must return and tell me. Then I may worship him also.

Magi: Yes, yes, certainly. *(They exit stumbling over their own feet and robes in their haste.)*

Narrator: Herod's advisor steps out from a curtain where he has been concealed during the entire interview. He hurries to Herod's side.

Advisor: Are you serious? Worship another king!

Herod: Whoever this king is . . . let the magi finish the task of finding him for me. Bethlehem holds nothing, but peasants. No one will miss a peasant child. Peasant children die every day. *(He smiles to himself.)* Now, hurry to the stables. See that the magi are properly taken care of.

Advisor: Yes, sire. *(He exits.)*

Narrator: Even the eagerness of the magi couldn't hurry the servants, who at the advisor's insistence, packed a week's provisions for the travelers. The sun was setting when their horses clattered out onto the stone streets of Jerusalem.

Melchior: *(Pointing upward)* Look, the star!

Narrator: Gazing upward they behold the star in its magnificence. It hung above them nearly speaking, 'this way, this way.'

Balthazar: It's leading us. Hurry we must follow!

Narrator: Urging their horses through the narrow streets of Jerusalem, the magi ride off on the few remaining miles of their quest.

ACT II

Scene 2

Narrator: After setting a steady pace for several hours, the horses instinctively slow to a trot, then stop entirely. The star has come to rest directly over a small house on the outskirts of Bethlehem. Hearing the approaching horses, a young woman looks out into the darkness. Few here have horses. Usually horses mean soldiers and Herod's soldiers bring trouble. What she saw instead were three, aged gentlemen dressed in royal robes.

Melchior: We have come to worship him whose star we have seen in the East — the newborn King of the Jews.

Narrator: Mary can not understand the words the visitors use, but their kindly faces put her at ease. She gestures toward the humble cradle.

(They dismount and enter.)

Balthazar: *(Triumphantly)* We have found him!

Kaspar: *(Reverently)* The Prince of Peace.

Narrator: All are visibly moved at the sight of the babe in these humble surroundings. Each falls to his knees and bows before the cradle. Mary stands in the shadows watching each magus involved in his own private worship of the child. After some time, Balthazar raises his head and speaks.

Balthazar: We have come many, long miles to bring our gifts to you.

38

Narrator: Each magus, in turn, reveals his gift and places it before the cradle. Mary softly steps from the shadows and offers food, but the magi are reluctant to leave the babe's side. Finally they pull their robes about them and doze. *(Hours pass)* At first light of dawn, the magi rise stiffly to leave — their visit has come to an end. After one last look into the cradle, they bow to Mary and leave the house. Their task is completed and yet, just begun. They must spread the joyful news to all, save Herod: The King has come!

www.ingramcontent.com/pod-product-compliance
Lightning Source LLC
Chambersburg PA
CBHW071759020426
42331CB00008B/2329

9 781556 733536